PRAISE FOR

DANCE AMONG ELEPHANTS

"Powerful Truths from eyes of an observer, who uses words succinctly the way he dances to make a statement of power. The flow of words once James Brown, once 'molam', once Rigor Mortis, once a crooner shows an extraordinary being sharing words we can heal from: From Laos to America."

— Dara Stieglitz, Lao American community builder

"Here before us is the debut of a startling young poet. Phounsiri's words will have you pivot from Laos and then uprock to San Diego and the San Francisco Bay Area. While reading these poems, a young man electrifies us with the exhilaration of dance, the uncertainties facing a young man in today's world, and the yearning for more love, singing, and joyful movement in this world. The poems for and about his family are at once heartbreaking and a testament to the persevering nature of the American immigrant story. These are poems documenting an American experience rarely put to print and often ignored or thought of as peripheral. Binly Phounsiri has proven, poem after poem, that his voice is creating his own path within American letters. We are all the better for such a passionate new young voice! I look forward to reading more and more of his fresh and invigorating words over the many years to come."

— Marcos Ramirez, artist and community builder

"A significant achievement for the next generation of Lao American writers and artists. An outstanding debut collection."

— Ketmani Kouanchao, Ed.D.

"It's an exciting text from a rarely heard perspective that will change the way many people see the Lao journey and more importantly, the Lao future."

— Nor Sanavongsay, author of *A Sticky Mess*

"Binly's vivid poetry takes you through pieces of his life that many Lao Americans can relate to. Dance Among Elephants is a must read."

— Chanida Phaengdara Potter, Founding Editor, *Little Laos on the Prairie*

Published by Sahtu Press
PO Box 907
Winchester CA 92596
email us@sahtupress.com

...

Dance Among Elephants / [written by] Krysada Panusith Phounsiri

Photos by Krysada Panusith Phounsiri
with the help of Joe Baiza and Kevin Tanoue.

Front Cover by Moshe Amundson

Book Layout by Nor Sanavongsay

Fonts are DIN Condensed and Cambria

ISBN: 978-0-9898850-2-7

SAHTU PRESS

DANCE AMONG ELEPHANTS

INDEX

SOUTHEAST

CITY OF FOG

MEKONG

THE THEATER

DEDICATED TO

My Father

My Mother

My Step Father

My Sister

My Brother

My Entire Family

My Crew

My Poetry for the People Group

Southeast San Diego

...

Marcos Ramirez

You were the person who read my words, heard my voice, and pushed me to write write write. Your fierce faith in my voice gave me the courage to love fearlessly through poetry. You inspired me to write my story as honest and as genuine as I am living it. This book is especially dedicated to you, so I begin the book with the very first poem I shared with you and our P4P group.

SOUTHEAST

ME AND MUSIC

Pounding bass
trembles my ribs
cymbals sizzle n drums juggle
captures me in a dark room
see nobody 'round me
snare hits
'Tat Boom'
my mind reading
invisible notes notifying me to
nod heads to Joe Bataan's horns
pop some funk with Rigor Mortis
givin' it up turnin' it loose with James Brown
damn that music takes me over
swaying of my body gives heat
melts the anchoring ice on my feet
with every bump
every beat
hips strutting with horns
while I swagger earthly rhythms
I see nobody
the waves of music
thrusting into me
adrenal energy
keeps the night young cuz
music paints the night black
and for me to walk away is for
me to say I'm wack
stepping on hours to pass
time now sleeps
this jam will last
after the music dies
wake me
from this trance
but now, I dance

MAMI TEACHES ME HOW TO WRITE

My Mother slides her fingers in
between my 4-year old right knuckles
cushions her palm around my hand to
guide each stroke curve and slash
all the while whispering
A   B   C
My fingers sail through this paper while I
grip my pencil
carving graphite as it moves
line to line going through a journey
navigating with my wrist
putting these letters together
like a puzzle that connects the
bars binding the two I's
to make an H
create a C and backward C
and the zig zag of the Z
If I can make my own puzzle
locking letters with
dots and sharp corners of V
I write the codes to fill this pasture
of letters
She whispers A B C
her hands hold mine
tingle the hair on my fingers
to keep my pencil moving
and we
sail deeper into the page

WHERE THE CURB CONNECTS

splashing
on the tints
of my 96' Honda Accord
you drip n sling
slow
down the driveway to the
sidewalk where
the curb connects
J St and Carlos St
so I name you
River of J Street

you muddy yourself
navigate grains
of concrete
towing dust
leaves and
pebbles from the asphalt
a murky body
reminding me of
the Mekong River
whose sands form brown
clouds underwater
waterway branches
that embed in borders
of the land
my mother births me in

I remember
plunging my hands
into the Mekong
cup its waters
as my skin tastes
this river
that my Aunt Ma Mon swims across
to a refugee camp

only to meet soldiers
with demands of sex
in exchange for admittance
as refugees

canal of my neighborhood
          drift
me
back to
the Mekong River
where Ao Thaun once
bathed me as a baby
holds my hand
as we walk the shores
that trail Mekong
because where the curb
ends
you become a brook
my new Mekong River
that unites
my dream
returning to the riverbed
of my home

SAXOPHONE SLING

days like this
speakers shush me
with woodwind sound
keep me company
under rooftops of white paint
as I look into bay area fog
past my window

past morning
mist on rims of my lips
no need for jogging my voice
saxophones from my speakers do the job

saxes sing jazz
as I post solo on my chair
let the room take me over
tune music loud
soon as saxophone slings come
my nose whiffs
fire from sax reed toots
down its bell mouth
Coltrane must be
a living metronome
attached to a sax
reminds me how
my curtain sway in wind

my loneliness quenches
in syncopation high-low chords
it feeds my ear
a belly now full
I need nothing more

POEM WHEN I NEED TO REMIND MYSELF TO LOVE

I droop
next to my dad
one morning
driving to
Ira Harbison Elementary
my 3rd grade lungs haggle
sobs
that carry over
from last night
when mom and dad
yell about
their disgust with living
together
another misunderstanding
as they fling shouts and shoves
slaps slip and slide
between their faces
physical dialogue
that happens soon
after Dad steps through
the door
3 a.m. after a party

four hours later
I sit in his truck
ask him
will you come back to us Dadi?
his stare, a drowsy
mash of weary looks
smoothing the tremble
in my voice
afraid he will leave forever
after he drops me off
he smiles
murmurs
No

and now
a decade later I ask
how the hell
can I love
afraid I too will ditch
the people I love

leave it with ease
fear it underneath my breath

then I smile
murmur
No

no matter
I will wake
next to my love
welcome her this morning
next morning
every morning
kiss and
kindle her neck
with my lips
every
brisk
lonely
morning
when the gap between the bed and our
hips need closure

I surrender myself
let love's river
waft me downstream
handcuff my worries plead for a hand
to smooth
the clefts of

this granite heart
that still loves
still loves

TO MY FATHER

To you, Dad, you work your whole life with your hands
You dislike violence, but you have to fight with your tough hands

You fight your frustration and work to pay for the books I read
With all your strength you operate printing machines; such might
with those hands

Permanent ink dries on your fingernails but you try to wash
them clean
I worry about your cut fingers, bandages tight on your scabby
hands

Dad, you tangle yourself helping grandpa and us kids,
Ease your troubles by singing songs holding the mic, gentle with
your hands

You work hours rough like your beard, you lose the ticks of time
Keep pushing overtime well into the night, with your sweaty
hands

One day, you stare into space while your fingers lay under the
blade machine
That paper guillotine slice, carve open blood fresh from your
hands

Dad, I will leave school so you can leave your job, let me take your
place
I can squeeze our worries about bills real tight, with my rough
hands

You say *Son, no problem I take care everything.*
I see your fingers caress keyboard keys all night, your strong
hands

DISH WASHER HANDS

We pour water
rub plates
pass time
conduct an orchestra
in a kitchen restaurant
rinsing dishes
plates that cling
chime the minimum wage
written in between
the hours
and when wet wrinkles of
skin dry and crack
the water
washes away
the tune plays
on repeat
soothing
the sounds
these hands create

STREET MASQUERADE

I have love at home
my love
massages mom and dad
on their backs and
shoulder blades
after long days of
late shifts of work
but my love
only lingers at home

when I leave my doorstep
a mask bolts to my face
as I walk down 47th and
Market
carrying with me
a profile:
young
southeast asian
male
deep affiliations with
local gangs
scoping corners for rival
gangs
who brawl

puberty broadens my
shoulders
I walk around
a moving target
men smirk bark
spit
mothafucka
where you from
betta watch your back
and even if I smile
even if I gesture

surrender myself in peace
wave a hand in the air
nah man I ain't from nothin
the words bounce off their
ears like a
brick basketball shot
no point for
friendship

I stay ready
fist clenching and in my mind
must decide when to
walk away or
wrench an arm
wreck the spine
with elbows to the neck
all while fearing
for my body

why must I
keep a low profile
why must I clinch my
eyebrows
hunch my shoulders
hide my
adam's apple with my chin
wonder why I gotta walk
like a foot soldier from
Imperial Ave
eyeing people
with a look
that makes my real friends
forget I ever smiled
I feel
no one outside my home
cares
to know my name or

where I come from or
what I love to do

I barely
walk just to enjoy the sun
as I stroll to
Malcolm X Library
always conscious when I
match certain colors because
people mean mug me
mistake my look as a threat
on their turf
and unless I hold the hand of my niece
or the hand
of my nephew
or walk my dog
only then can I skip on the
sidewalks with the
breeze
as the only thing hitting my face

I want to unscrew
my street mask
crush it to the asphalt
no more cold stares
shut lips
I just want to strut
up and down
Southeast San Diego
and let this town embrace me
like the love I leave at home

STARS IN SOUTHEAST

Child

you the star
that knows
how lamps glow
dim in rooms
saves electricity
cuz costs of bills so hot
they burn your mommy and daddy's eyes

you the star
that no one
outside Market Street
and Imperial Avenue
wants to see shine
yet you graffiti murals
of hood hero faces
tag your name
of friends passed away

no one cares of your light
beyond this galaxy
of police sirens
and helicopters
hovering the sky
intruding your sleep
along with drive-bys and
shoot outs at high schools
the nay sayers
dare cup you with their hands
you sear through its cracks
with what you write
and write you must do
as if your story flickers
flames more flashing than supernovae

illuminate
the spirit
of your every day
on walls
backsides of car repair shops
on the plane of paper
you a star in Southeast
warm this Earth
that needs to know
how you can glow
in a room of night
let the world marvel at you

STELLA

A summer day
slips between
the hands of my
living room clock
as I slide
into sheets
of a bed in my garage
I know no outside heat
no fire of Mom's scolding
to my brother
not cleaning his room
no flame from
my sister and brother
fighting about gas money
driving to school
thirteen miles away
no sun skin frying rays
can play tag in my garage

my baby puppy
Stella sniffs the scent of
my feet
nudging to
make room
hopping onto my bed
I look at her eyes
and I want to
lunge through her vision
dig into her mind
and plant a memo
so I can whisper
I wish you never leave me
you make me
forget I ever hear people yell
I can lay on the bed
while laying my troubles

on the floor
my worries about if
any girl will call me for dinner
doesn't scratch my skin
Mom and Dad can go
argue somewhere else
my boys can find
another place
to get down n dance

my world for that moment
involves me and Stella
everybody who got heat
can
       chill outside
because I only surrender
to the warmth
of Stella
her nose
a perfect fit under
my ribs

I don't care
if the whole world
freezes before me
I just need
Stella there
she melts the
cold rhythms of my day

ODE TO THE BREAK BEAT

you fumble wild sounds
bump air
beneath earth
rumble like burps of thunder
when hit with sticks
on leather
Kool Herc calls you
the break beat
percussion solo
you carry bones
of Candido funk
sound of snares
bells chimes basses
and calypso tint
flicker fire in legs
of Bboys and Bgirls
whose hips and bottoms
mimic drum thumps
your rhythms steal legs
of anyone feeling your patterns
n rock them legs dancing day away
listen to the funky drummer
JB's juggle drums patterns
back to New Orleans
back to the birth of Jazz
rifts
rocket our ears
blasts us back to Africa
mother of the break beat
you drift us to meet
your cousin drums of Zulu
huehuetl of Aztecs
rattles of Cheyenne
gongs from Lue villages
and their dancers wind
into the way you strut

I play the Apache track
loud for neighbors
to bob their heads
thread that DJ needle
into vinyl
my body melds
into you

a climax
of cymbal hiss
conga bobble n snare sputters
I ride you
heart throb of music
lovely
till I feel
the hands of
drummers
pat my cheek
hands that strike drums
hands that flick on any surface
just to get a tat ta tat tat
a boom bap
break my body into
measures of music
where you batter
lineage of music of my people
Bboys and Bgirls warrior-dancers
of Lue Juern
anyone who speaks music
with their arms flinging
elbows swiveling circles
to your command
you soothe
till I feel nothing
but the song
and my body
bouncing

BROTHER

I write this poem for you
we got ethnic funk
with each other
the type of funk
that floors the gas pedals
of bullet spitting cars

bullets and shell powder
decorate our homes

funk that reeks
from my grandpa Oo Pa's
million memories
of the Vietnam War
and refugee bodies that sink
down rivers
the massacres of Khmer Rogue
killing fields of Secret War in Laos
the endless U.S. Bombings
like sands n rocks
of our countries
turn upside down
falling from the sky

when we shout
Flea
Roach
Ah-Meo

guns slip up from our belt straps
as we bang and name claim our blocks
as we bang
our fist into
each other's eye sockets
we insult

each other's home
our words drag
the dying breath
of our lungs
like a bullet
that howls
and hacks through
the throat of a Glock
our hate for each other
binds us to the
asphalt

we dry rice roots in the sun
no space for the wetness
of love for all our people
in America
where we learn to hate
other Southeast Asians
not like our own

so I offer you
another name
a name
I pull from
rice baskets
a sticky rice name
that shapes
on the roofs of your mouth
warms your stomach
coal for the furnace
of your belly
that fires you
in the coldest of nights

how about
I call you
Aye or Nong
Bong or own

caw
Anh
big brother, little brother

we become vagabonds
who sail an ocean
to harbor ourselves
in our motherland
where we know
our skin shades
brown like the puddles
of summer rain
in Hanoi
we have to look into each other's eyes
the moisture
traces back to
our mother and
our mother's motherland
our father
and our father's fatherland

I need to write a poem
and post it
on every sticky note
graffiti this poem
on all *stop* signs
and walls that surround
middle schools n high schools
of our city
I need to scratch this poem
on the windows
of the apartments
the duplexes
the rented homes
of my southeast asian brother

no longer
will we

waste breath
on hate

CITY OF FOG

DINNER PICKINGS

there exists
no haven
to hide
no shelter
to shield
no barricade
to defend
myself from
loving you

your focus on me
smashes any fear
of rejection
into seeds
for my pomegranate heart
that I throw
freely
into the world
for you to catch

I pluck my life stories
and gather my time like
berries in my hands
as you plant words
inside the soil of conversation
stories you want
to grow with time
riches we carry to dinner
where we share
my pickings
where we savor
each other's stories
bite by bite

AHMAD JAMAL – I LOVE MUSIC

Ahmad see-saws
off the cadence of his fingers
pressed on
            black
and white
            keys
of his piano
the song plays
in the background

peach lipstick lips
dig for jazz inside me
composed by my lover
I mimic Ahmad's song
glide my fingers
on her piano tummy
breathe staccato on
each other's skin
then switch to legato
hair tangles like
bass and treble
sway in the trance of bodies
they speak of what loving
music brings
we care not about outside gloom
her lips trace the slow tempo of mine
making love
through this song
grasping whatever jazz
we can find

RAIN

fate   floats
                                        like the rain
            just a sprinkle
                                    mist that
scatters
            the sky
                                                a beautiful time
                                    to
            be drifting
                                wherever
the wind
            pleases
                                                and the journey
runs
                                    wild
                        in mid-air
            no floors to
push back
                                                        no walls
                                                        confine
                        I spin
shift speeds
                                    all the rain
                        drops
            cry
                        live
without
            fears
                        of

                        falling

BRISK WIND, PART 1

she plays her guitar
we improvise
voices hum
for the first time
singing
whatever flows
out our minds
we ask
about our names
what we like
whatever flows
out our minds
her humming hits me
and nights like this
never shy to the background until
it sees her red lips
take center stage
where we sit

she invites me over
later that week
to teach me
how to bake desserts
I accept her invitation
her aroma
catches me
like a gust of sunshine
after a winter storm

BRISK WIND, PART 2

we massage cookie dough
sugar and vanilla
I slow myself
witness the work of her beauty
drip between her fingers
her engagement ring
watches me on the counter
I know not to cross
the bond of their love

bake myself into
the moment
indulge in any food
she offers
we keep each other
in conversation
doused in the sugar
of her voice
while the cookies
ready in the oven
the lemon bar batter
waits on the dining table
we bake slow
as the night
heats the kitchen
with me and her in it

MELINDA

Inspired by "Stan Getz & Bill Evans – Melinda"

the name itself
makes enough music
to convince me
to love her
Me-lin-da
I breathe the city nights of
Downtown San Diego
as the harbor lifts the smell of salt
thick
in the air like
a saxophone reed
just enough ring in vocal chords
and licks with a tongue
to keep me dreaming
through this song

LOVE IN DECEMBER

my love
reads 45 degrees
winter
walk
hands clinching
cold air
weather
makes my
cheeks
heat up
each time a
breath blows
fog
overcast
from your lips

BRISK WIND, PART 3

Coit Tower never been
a place that matters
until we walk
there together
a whole day woven
by strolls on sidewalks
through the heart
of fog city

Your skin fluoresced
as if the moon
cares to light only you
we stare at the bay
being here quilts all
that soothes
quilts
all things lovely
with the present

I keep words to myself
lick my chapped lips so they stay busy
want to stay with you
as long as this tower stands
but no confession makes it
past the barrier of night
between my mouth
and your ears
just a silence and us
sitting shoulder to shoulder
I will pretend we sat there forever

COMING BACK

forecasts mutter
tomorrow will rain
drops will dive
down cement
and applaud
patter
descending
it is the sky's way
of accepting
your journey
back to me

INSTRUCTIONS FOR WARMTH IN BED

snuggle your feet
between the ends of
your bed sheet and blanket
have your calves hold
each other
rub them so they nestle
center yourself
on your belly
huddle knees to chest
clasp hands
on thighs
crease the top of your blanket
around the rim of your neck
that way heat circles
from your heels
to your head
lastly
pretend she holds you
somewhere surrounding
your body
cold
believe
this heat
comes from her

WHATEVER'S LEFT

I want you
like an Earth
wants its sky
with clouds in
the same plane like
a child wants a Sun
beaming over their
cheeks when they
skate 'round the block like
a neighborhood
wants the feet
of its people
walking its asphalt
like sidewalks want
flowers by its side
on days no one plays
outside like
the times clouds rain
over your shoulders
and I want to
wipe the rain drops
off with my lips
like the water
wants to moist
my wanting of you
so no cracks
on my skin
have only themselves
as company

and
whatever
remains
in my world
of wants
wishes the day
wants

you

and I
in it

MEKONG

A BREATH OF SOUTHEAST IN MY MOTHER'S WOMB

Southeast sky in Huay Xai Lao
dive into my mother's lungs and
into my bagpipes of life
a Southeast Sky that the Sun
sneaks light through to
peek pass the thick fog
witness the signs of my birth

Sometimes remnants of cinder
warm the morning chills
Mother breathes the smoke
I take whatever air
my Mother breathes
and kick so she knows
the cinder rouses me

She immerses herself in the Mekong River
cleanses her skin letting each molecule
glide 'round her body
water drops that get lucky
swim down her throat
into her womb and
streams with my body
I taste the Mekong River for the
first time

My mother's womb
moist like the lakes
that bathe her
I swim in
this sphere of birth
so good
I call myself selfish if
I ever learn to
swim like that
again

Time comes for me to
leave my mother's brook
pass the nurturing canal
and I meet the Southeast sky
for the first time
born
in the corner of
a wooden house
guarded by green groves and
bamboo brush
on the second floor
in the corner of my mother's room

My jerks and kicks and squints
worry my mother
one breath and
I cry
the sacred air inside
escapes
time to inhale with
two nostrils like
caves on my face

Southeast air
pouched in jewels
leave their marks in my lungs
with the tinge of smoke still fresh
from the cinder
I believe the
weight of my spit still
reminds me
to inhale every spec of
Huay Xai sky
forever unite with
the world I trap in my
little bagpipes

In my mother's river
In my mother's sky
In my mother's home for me

ODE TO KAO NIEW

I meet you in Laos
as a seed
just a simple
existence of hard rice
seeded inside Huay Xai's dirt
until water plains
cradle and nourish your infant body
'till you sprout above water banks
where you tickle yourself
with sunshine
like a child who spends all
day with the wind
when you mature
people pull your roots
carry you in bulk back home
along with your friends
moisten your skin
steam under flames and
boiling water
only a bath where
dirt splashes off
while you try to hold
breaths underwater
your skin does not wrinkle
only softens
to stick with other rice
and sink in perfection
of the basket
where my mother's hands
shake and shuffle you
into a ball
to roll on a plate
now fully grown ready to
liberate our hunger
with your body
that is how we meet

everyday even now
when I chew you in big bites
you never fail to fill
my head with steam
and make my tummy your
cozy home
sometimes I eat you too fast
you burn my tongue

and mom says
I am crazy for eating too fast
but it don't matter
when I can cool
squeeze to pebble-size bits
dip you in fish soup
or papaya salad
Kao Niew
my family sits together
on the floor legs folded
or on a dinner table
you cuddle inside our bellies
warm our lips
all
        the way
        down
our throats
in cold evenings with no heaters
you sacrifice to
fill our stomachs
so we can stick to each other
and swallow
our love whole

IT BEGINS WITH A HAUNTING

a ghost haunts the country of Laos
sieving through jungles
crackling twigs because
it has not yet died
beware of it
the one who drags one foot
while the other rots 20 feet away
shoes made of cast metal
footprints ever so present
in night fall
imprints of bomb shells in mud fields

a phantom roams
plains in Laos
hide your children
its breath reeks of agent orange
its shouts
dynamite flames that dusts away human bones
and bamboo baskets
a stench of wheezing willing to fold
       curl
leaves and skins of families who
who hide in forest
till their flesh shrivels
like the lungs of many dead soldiers

the fissures of its face
exposes land mines
crooning a song of torment
through throats of civilians fleeing
on the hair of this
wicked phantom
its hair droops the length
of the Ho Chi Minh trail
hear its whispers

it also cries
moans of a past that begs
to be remembered
clawing trees to spell out its name

the ghost wails pain
filters itself everywhere
whimpering
peeling steel and lead
by the millions
what remains become chains
that burrow into earth
by cluster bombs
big bombs
B-52 bombers dropping
in its tons of U.S. congress approval
in ink
an old friend still alive and well

and under moonlight
refugees run
only to meet more trouble
in camps
they desire to break away
from this ghost and its name
and no one recalls its name
of this

ghoul who rages through
the country of

Laos

melting tendons and flesh
this ghost hungers
for humans
screeching napalm gas on
palms of

guerilla soldiers
american soldiers
and vietcong alike
death does not even remember its name

beware but
tell your children
light the candles and the incense
the ghost drifts because no one wants to
know about its name

The Secret War

put this crying soul
of secret history
to rest
recognize
its name
bless this curse
that wants to
name
all the people
it claims
and they too
will remain alive
like mines beneath the soil
seeds of calamity

NIMBLE

For Oo Pa, my Grandfather

I wonder if
as a child,
our play fights would be the same
without your fat
relaxing under your skin

If each pound
a piece of jolliness
trickles off in sweat
a 1973
Re-education camp kind
of sweat
muddy from the
rice fields kind of sweat
away from a family bed
for years kind of sweat
a thinness you never showed me
memories hidden in your wrinkles

Can't imagine you
        skinny,
needed your belly sides
plump
so I could climb your back
arms wrapped
feet desperate to
perch on your shoulders
you'd dodge my kicks
waltz your weight
on your tip toes
one stride to another
laugh and roar
like you had a trunk and tusks

I mimic your moves
keep them on Earth
while you dance with Oo Ma
off this world,
each step
a piece of jolliness
you left with me

FATHER, HOW YOU CAPTURE ME

this night
I ask you to perform
a song
you un-sheath
your Espada
this guitar
whose tunes
coax Mami one time long ago

your hands scuff a chord
playing old songs from
Laos with long notes
low pitches
your fingers rattle
guitar rifts
the strings
make a chime
that lobs in air
music unlocks a new
picture of you

you don't look
like a printer anymore
wrinkles on your face
fade away
bags under your eyes
like valleys
flatten out into plains
cheek bones
rock hard
I see the twenty year old in you
whose hair lengthens
long enough
for Mami to play
her fingers shuffle

a slight swish

through your hair

it makes a song

I breathe in tempo
devour morsel acoustics
my mind crafts
a memory for my
heart to carry

Dad you strum life
into the guitar
the harmony
lands on my ear drum
like ripples in water
nothing soothes my body more
than your fingers flicking
chords
so swiftly

THE RACE

Pistols shoot
and rifles unload
thunderous banters
initiate the race
she dives
into the Mekong River
stealth head start
she leads amongst the pack
of four boys and three girls
paddles faster than catfish

other swimmers dive
chasing for the finish line
the Thailand border
no one trains for this race
many do not know
how to swim
instincts ignite energy
in their arms and legs
signals their brain to
pick up the skill
on the spot

faces
splash into
murky depths
greeting a timezone
between breath
and drowning
some legs fail to flap
some racers sink
and one boy gives up
swims back to Laos
the rest continue
down to Paiyanag's home
death cries with people

underwater
either bullets pierce their
flesh or the
breathing
seizes
water filling lungs

100 meters
200 meters
400 meters
her Olympic debut
two hours long
she peeks ahead
sand and shore
on the horizon
her feet do not give up
her hands
cup away whispers
to submerge beneath the Mekong
she ignores temptation
to call it quits
the finish line waits at
Nong Khai refugee camp

no one cares
where they place
first or second
or last as long
as their knees can
sink into dry earth
rather than their corpses
be fish food
she crawls
out the Mekong River
looks back
at her homeland torched
ammo shells whizzing
no audience present

no cheers

no celebration
only the moon
and the stars
watching her
speed
tracking her velocity
until the finish line
her medal for winning
Prison

then,
a new Life

in America

WHITE ROSE SLAP

For Oo Ma, My Grandmother

I.
Oo Ma loves to pluck
white rose petals and place
them on her left palm
she shows me the petals
looking like it shines as it
rests on her hand
now she slaps it with her
right hand and it
rips in the middle
what looks to be alive a
second ago
dies

II.
In my backyard
radiance in the sky blankets the
groggy afternoon
daylight and darkness
go hand and hand

my fingers cling to bike chains
greasy to the fingerprint
as I try to
fix the chain
then someone calls from
the house and
I walk in
family grown-ups huddle around
Oo Ma who
lays on the bed
she can't be sleeping
this time of the day
I see her stare at the ceiling
I walk close and

the grown-ups tell me to
stay away
I don't listen to them
I glare at the whites of
Oo Ma's eyes the whites
of her gown the
white
of her face

the living room space full with
faces that pour
tears so wet I can
bathe in their eyelids

I stare at Oo Ma

she breathes – and gurgles
breathes – and gurgles

why are you not breathing?
tell me why you ignore the
spit that grips your throat as you
try to breathe

she answers my thoughts
with one last breath

her last breath
keeps me from crying
but my mother weeps
the sound of it
drowns me

I gaze at Oo Ma and I feel
how fast a white rose petal
dies

and how one slap can tear
its life
and memories rip

Oo Ma's last breath
blooms out my lungs
with every sigh

AFTERLIFE

For Oo Ma

I look
for a cricket
hope it appears
in a corner
of our home
Mami used to
hush us kids
tell us to
bow our heads three times
"It's Oo Ma" she whispers

I search for
her soul
pray she follows us
from rented home
to rented home
must have been
her spirit
that sparks the incense
with the whiff
of a flame
ashes fall when we recite sutras

I bend my legs
weight on my knees
don't care if I must crouch
inside my closet
or lay on the Event Horizon
of a Black Hole
I still look for a cricket
that hops its way
into my travels
listen for a chirp
like a lullaby
Oo Ma used to sing

MEMENTO OF A HUAY XAI WOMYN

If the roof planks
in my Mother's old home
catch second chance
at life
they would sprout
flowers in Red White
and Blue
moisturized in afternoon mist
embellishing
the moment she swears
her allegiance to America

and when the petals bloom
they will rip into
twenty three pieces
for every year my Mother
sleeps in a land
she tries her best
to call her own
dreams of the day
her children
will find solace
in the Land of the Free
away from selling vegetables
in the village market
like she used to in Laos

Should the whiff of petals
surface on the Mekong River
it will glow Red White and Blue
the town of Huay Xai cheers
for the two hundred seventy six months
that she devises a plan
to bring food home
and keep the shower running hot
no indication of giving up hope

invade my Mother's mind
nowhere present in her first job
boxing light bulbs
nowhere present when she opens
her Lao gift shop

as the aura of colors
engage the earth beneath her
my Mother can laugh
at the times she asks
for the spelling of a street name
pray to thank Buddha
for every customer
who buys from her shop
and smile while finally holding
her Citizen Certificate
the way she smiles
relieves the weight
of pipe dreams
crushing her back because finally
she is American
the oath she recites
the paper greeting her hand
inform her
she is American
reinforced by the eight thousand
seven hundred sixty five days
of living in San Diego
preparing for this day to come

My Mother can gladly call
America her own
on a February day
inside the Chula Vista Naturalization Office
though her heart
will forever
carry her homeland
wherever she may be

SA BAI SA BAI

you ever heard of a Lao party?
might be one going on right now...
we Lao folks love that celebratin'
sifting through sunrise and slipping
through sunset we sing our favorite
songs in our heads
it shortens time at work
cuz we sa baiiii sa baiiii
we force ourselves to
sa bai through the weekdays
so when weekend come
we too sai bai to be sa bai while
Beer Lao gushes down as if a recession
exists in our bellies
and we must stimulate our celebratory economy
this weekend on our little cousin's birthday where grandpas and
grandmas
get down Salavan style
Lao folks gotta play that music
gives us an excuse to pick up microphones
clap our hands and wave our wrist around
and dance like how our aunties teach us
when the right song come
when the right keys
of the khaen flute lifts our stress out
our sleepless bodies
we always celebrating something
waiting for that weekend
coasting past the jobs we hate
or waiting to grab jobs we don't have
it don't matter if our elders can't speak English
they singing like they own the land
where their voices reach
rejoicing over the smallest
of happenings
and we all sa baiiii real good

THE THEATER

CHINK IN THE ARMOR

To Anthony Federico and Other Writers who want
to use the word "Chink"

I am a chink
by definition of
the slur slinging
from generations of
"orientals" before me

the chink
who mines through
a Gold Rush California
for 6 dollars a month
and gets taxed 3 dollars

the chink
who could not legally marry
anyone except chinks
before 1967

the chink
sent to Internment camps
because the army
cannot tell the difference
between any Asian chink

the chink whose name echos
from the end of Ronald Eben's
baseball bat to Vincent Chin's skull
from the ears of Private Danny Chen
dragged across yards of gravel
by his sergeant
rocks pelt his body
while comrades
yell
chink
gook

dragon-lady
he blasts his face after wards
shotgun blasts ringing
suppresses his hearing
escaping the echos

the chink
that people call a gook
the Lao
Cambodian
and Vietnamese refugees
forgotten in
a war of
Rambo versus little yellow Viet Cong men

the chink
who yells
ching chong lin long tin tong
in libraries across state campuses
where my hard work
and Confucian principles
make me study my
model minority ass off
only to fail at physics and math
then somehow graduate
with enough
knowledge of words
to inform you
Mr. Federico
that your remark
exhausts the stupidity of
every human being
whose ignorance
costs a life
taxed with racial beating
you should mend
the battered pieces
of your own armor

"POETRY IS ALWAYS FOR THE PEOPLE AND IT IS ALWAYS A TIME OF WAR."

– RUTH FORMAN

If we poets
be in time of war
then let me write
these poems
rip them
      thread them
tape them
press them as tourniquets
on wounded people

death bangs the doors
of any block or town
any place where weapons
itch the palms of men
one mortar missile one
bullet crack in brain
one hand clasp on
neck one rifle butt
bat swing to the cranium
can snap any civilian
to dust
a sight too familiar
for people in Gaza

soldiers
in Gaza
strap on
water proof
cut proof cry
proof
black laces up to the shin
boots
Palestinian children
strap on sandals or shoes
that bear weight of

human beings
who want to live

I want to fold
the pages of my
poems
with them
wrap
the right arm of a mother
cut from metal
after a missile explodes
thrashes a fire tantrum
on a town
or crease these poems
around a foot of a boy
who greets blight
by blast

these poems
do no
justice
if they sit on paper
I wish
this paper
can plug flesh wounds
this red wine blood
gushing like tidal waves
on the sands in Gaza

A TOAST WITH DAD, POST-DIVORCE

Father, may I
share with you recollections
we possess of each other
it will help me sleep better

How come I never see fingerprints
on keyboard keys
your fingers
be canvases, where ink
smothers in crevices of your fingernails
my eyes look in awe
rather hear you play music at home
than through frequency
and synths of a cell phone call

Father, do you
remember treading to work after
you scold me
I don't remember what for
this child-father quarrel
ends when you exit a door
and me doing 50 push-ups
tears slide down my navel as I
squeeze my torso shutting air
imprison my sobbing
inside my rib cage
never wanting to smash fist with you
you return home later
hours at work strip
hours you worry about me
like the socks you slip off
your feet
lying beside stairs

Father,
you sometimes say

you need to be   alone
deadlines of flyers or books or pamphlet
production
you look
exhausted,
family care evolves to family troubles
especially with Mom
challenges nerves
of keeping us five together
you desire relaxation
permanent vacation in Laos
you rub my psyche
blank

You and I both like to shut up
rather pin our focus on work
and the people we do it for
cleanse everything unnecessary
I know why you taste freedom
in a shot glass of Black Label whiskey
I now do the same,
I know why your eyes look drowsy
fantasizing day and night
about staring at stars in Laos
where you can play the keyboard
make more of your own songs
memories of your American dream
dilute in whiskey you drink

Father,
may I still call you Daddy?
Will you save all our memories
leave none behind
please save me days
I can toast repeatedly
for all lessons you teach me
of dreaming alone

drinking to our soul's content

or we can remember
nothing

but each other's faces
sharing the same grin
that speak volumes
of love
without words

both drowsy
reflections
that move us along

COURT HEARING FOR THI

March 17th, 2008
Finally they say, they will release him!
correctional officers give him green light
news of sun and pollen
outside his bars
he is free to go
pack your things
they say

his hands had to be busy
packing
folding what clothes he might have even the sweat stays warm
from the arms that tingle
they become anxious to greet
his mother
after the planned drive
from Phoenix to Visalia

but in one fax
from Governor Arnold
he says no
sends a fax
to Thi's one home
out of many prisons
where he lays
his side on
he will keep Thi
kissing steel bars

Thi speaks with
solemn eyes
admits
that be the first time
they break him
in all sixteen years in jail

they finally break him
even after they stamp
DEPORTED
on his record
but couldn't send him back to Laos
sea to shining sea salt tears glisten on his eyes

he tells me of prison life
shares little with me
his days in a Thai refugee camp
Do they feel the same?
He internalizes home
in four corner cement
a box behind bars
injects thoughts of forever being criminal
but always hoping for freedom

a few months
out of prison
his laughter
bangs the four corners
of his room
tells the story
in the warmth of his own bed
freedom does him well

WHITE WALLS

last night
lust pushes us
into each other's
hands coaxed
behind the backs
of our heads
love locks
our lips
and the words
lust and love
mean the same

we sweat
lather skin
in perspiration
ribs rock and
our hips row naked
beneath blankets

but tonight
I stare at her walls
dry of any sweat
like the night before

her nose cuddles in sheets
no warmth teases my neck
our bodies cities apart
I long to feel her
goosebumps again

she pushes me away
when I want to hold her
no longer do I feel
I slept with the same person
and thoughts fester on whether

she ever cared about
our escapade

I desperately look
at this wall
uninspired
needing to forget
lust and love altogether

SIN CITY, PART 1

this desert
a crystal ball city
covers me in sand
flashing billboards
and hotels
too many to name

winds toss me
they do not forgive
the ounces
of alcohol I drink
after dancing on stage
every night
the buzz sways my mood
from glamour decoration in
night clubs
believing the
soreness of
my body fade away

this city
drains me as fast
as the cinder creeping
down cigarettes of gamblers
no one knows who I am
they come and go
in this desert
blown around by winds

WHEN I DANCE

I seize time when funky drummer songs break
into my body robbing feeling of nerves making me fly
off floors with hips bouncing and shoes sweeping soot on
concrete
I leave my history on any ground wherever I scuff my hands and
greet earth beneath me made of cement and sand roughening
calluses in

my upper palm and never do I feel more alive in
doing anything other than breaking
dancing on the floor that my fingers sand
with blood thrashing through my veins till I push and fly legs
flailing toward the moon; only my hands
feel this field of concrete

within the hour, ridges of concrete
rub against my knuckles as I guzzle in
air gasping for breaths that hit my hands
feeling this warmth pat me does nothing more than break any
possibility that I might be dreaming, flying somewhere or dead
drifting with sand

dirt smears its calligraphy in an ink of sand
when my shoes scrape concrete
markings on the floor inscribe stories and time flies
I see scratches my palms and shoes make in
a canvas of floors where I dance till the break
of dawn meditating with music, the bandage of my hands

I read life through my hands
brush rubble or throw sand
dancing off feelings of being lonely breaking
nostalgia of home because I can find that in concrete the ground
teaches me of pain on my skin or inside
my mind as I wander into a song flying
and falling over pebbles that gash my flesh blood flying

all directions and while wiping blood from my hands

I feel my age seeping the years I keep anxiety in
on a path of exhaustion counting thuds of my heart with
sandpaper
hands I forge on concrete
I will slide-spin-tap the floor in harmony breaking

my life into stories of me dancing in all worlds I touch, showing
the world my broken
rhythm in handling pain with hands pressed on floors people
walk on in concrete
cities where I fly into freedom, puffing out, dying breaths, and
taking all, breaths of life, in

SIN CITY, PART 2

Nights I work
in the theater
leaves crowds
clapping
applause pounce
life back into my ears
I live for it
such sounds finish too soon
'round midnight
people go off in their ways
doing things
they can't do
at home
and I find myself
drifting
in a 24 hour city
its clubs do not
console me
its money likes to leave me
its people
I sit down with at
my favorite bar
beer chills
down my throat
empty bottles clink
in trash bins
hits me harder than
the music playing
under Vegas lights
substitutes for Sunlight

I stay
long enough
for lights
to turn off

sleep when the Sun
hikes down the mountains
and wake when
this crystal ball shakes
and night arrives and I work
in the theater
living to make crowds
leave clapping
bottles clinking
in the distance

STREAM IN THE SIDEWALK

Inspired by Li-Young Lee

In the city
where I love you
the roads wait and has waited
for your return
these footsteps
of mine stomp
through streams in the rain
in search
for a face
with your name

in this city
where I love you
your lipstick smears
red as my ears when you
hug me
this bliss
dusts my jacket
never will I drench it

this city holds me
when you disappear
then throws me out when
I find you again
rids me of
my face
when I call for you
and the wind whistles nothing
I live in this city
that much
I know
its name matters not
only your hand
a petal in my grasp

you press my collar
as we kiss
travel endless
sidewalks of our mouths
our tongues become
navigators
inside blankets
where I love you
where no country can shed
its borders on us
we sail through
blues of my blanket
Night emerges
I almost faint
while dancing with you
scavenging your sweat
resting my nose on yours
I inhale
the city
this corner of land
of home in the brown
of your skin

when you pull my hands
to your breasts
I feel the fog of the city
and I rather be lost in this night
with no answers to where
I need to go
keeping each other awake
longer than train rides
and street lights

only when I enjoy our love
solemn vindication of summer
will I know
these hands belong to me
but you can keep them

cling threads
of your hair
that I don't have
astray in pavements
when you disappear
streams pouring into sidewalks
never forgetting to keep
your reflection
ceaseless
downstream

and I wait
for a sign to smile
for all the ways
you return

ELEPHANT DANCER

I offer my body
as a kingdom
where you
can take refuge

form pathways
smoothing the earth
of my belly
where people can
lie their heads on
stroll up to my chest
hike to reach down to my hands
where we can fold our
fingers together

Shade yourself
under my hug
feel my diaphragm
an accordion that
exhales ambiance
of sunset
warmth that makes me
croon
songs of
my world
elephant chant
through my kingdom
where you
can find home
with my skin and my words
my words
my
words

watch me
dance

among Elephants
it will rock you
'till the world shakes
all its leaves
to the ground

ABOUT THE AUTHOR

Krysada Panusith Phounsiri, better known as "Binly" is a Lao-American Artist and Engineer. He was born in Laos in 1988 and immigrated to America with his family in 1989. Binly graduated from UC Berkeley in 2010 with a Physics & Astrophysics Double Major and a Minor in Poetry. His creative work has appeared in the *Journal of Southeast Asian American Education and Advancement*, *Little Laos on the Prairie*, and also at the Smithsonian Asian Pacific American Center.

A resident of San Diego, he pushes his passion for dancing, mainly the Hip Hop Street Dance known as Breaking, by traveling to various regions of the world to compete in competitions and teach workshops. He is also involved in developing the Snap Pilots Photography Project; a venture he and a friend created.

ABOUT SAHTU PRESS

Sahtu Press was established in 2013. Their mission is to publish and promote enduring contemporary Lao American literature and to create academic and grassroots learning opportunities. It was officially recognized as a 501 (c) 3 non-profit organization in 2015.

Sahtu Press acquires, publishes, and markets high quality, imaginative work from emerging and established Lao American writers or those working on issues of interest to the Lao American community.

You can visit them online at www.sahtupress.com

NOTES: